The Meat and Fish Cookbook for My Lean and Green Diet

50 special and delicious Meat and Fish recipes for your Lean and Green diet, to burn fat fast and stay healthy

Josephine Reed

Table of contents

Shrimp cucumber bites

Total time: 60 minutes

Serve: 6

Ingredients:

- 1/3 cup olive oil
- ¼ cup lime juice
- 2 tbsp. honey
- 2 cloves garlic (minced)
- 1 tsp. Cajun seasoning
- ½ tsp. salt (divided)
- 1 lb. shrimp (peeled, deveined, and tails discarded)
- 2 avocados
- 2 tbsp. lime juice
- ½ onion (finely minced)
- 1 jalapeño (finely chopped)
- 2 tbsp. coriander (chopped, plus more for garnish)
- 2 cucumbers (sliced ½ inch thick)

Instructions:

1.Combine the oil, lime juice, sugar, garlic, and the Cajun seasoning in a dish. With salt, season. Attach the shrimp and toss until thoroughly coated, then cover and leave for 30 minutes or up to an hour to rest in the fridge.

2.Take a pan and place it over medium heat, cook shrimp until pink (about 2 minutes per side). Remove from heat.

3.Meanwhile, in a bowl, mash avocados, add lime juice, red onion, jalapeño, coriander, and stir to combine. Season with the remaining salt.

4.On each cucumber slice, put a tablespoon-sized amount of guacamole.

Savory coriander salmon

Total time: 110 minutes

Serve: 4

Ingredients:

- 4 cups coriander (divided)
- 2 tbsp. lemon/lime juice
- 2 tbsp. hot red pepper sauce
- 1 tsp. cumin
- ½ tsp. salt (divided)
- ½ cup of water
- 4, 7 oz. salmon filets (raw)
- 2 cups yellow bell pepper (sliced)
- 2 cups green bell pepper (sliced)
- ½ tsp. black pepper
- cooking spray

Instructions:

1.In a food processor, put half of the coriander, lemon or lime juice, hot red pepper sauce, cumin, salt, and water, and blend until smooth. Transfer the marinade to a resealable plastic bag.

2.Add salmon to marinade. Seal the bag by squezing out the air; turn it to coat the salmon. Let it rest in the fridge for 65 minutes, turning the bag now and then.

3.Meanwhile, preheat the oven to 410°F. Arrange pepper-slices in a single layer in a lightly-greased baking tray, and sprinkle with black pepper and the remaining salt. Bake for 23 minutes, turning pepper slices once.

4.Drain salmon, and discard the marinade. Crust tops of salmon with the remaining fresh coriander. Place salmoon on top of pepper slices, and bake until fish flakes easily when tested with a fork (about 12-14 minutes).

Grilled shrimp skewers

Total time: 35 minutes

Serve: 1

Ingredients:

- ¾ lb laarge shrimp (raw)
- green pepper (cut into thick chunks)
- 1 cup whole mushrooms
- ½ tsp Old Bay seasoning
- tbsp. roasted red pepper vinaigrette

Instructions:

1.Marinate the shrimp in the roasted red pepper vinaigrette for 30 minutes (discard dressing).

2.Alternate shrimp, peppers, and mushrooms on a skewer.

3.Grill skewers on foil, turning once.

4.Sprinkle shrimp with Old Bay seasoning.

Salmon and asparagus with peppers puree

Total time: 40 minutes

Serve: 1

Ingredients:

- 6 oz. raw salmon
- 1 cup fresh asparagus
- ¼ cup red bell peppers (diced)
- ¼ cup raw tomatoes (diced)
- 1/8 tsp. salt
- ½ cup water
- 2 tbsp. red wine vinegar
- cooking spray
- ¼ tsp. pepper

Instructions:

1.Preheat oven to 350° F.

2.Dice the tomatoes and peppers; spray lightly with some cooking spray on a cookie sheet.

3. Season both sides of the salmoon lightly with salt and pepper. Place the salmon in a baking dish and add water to the baking tray.

4.Bake for about 22-24,5 minutes with the salmon and vegetables.

5. For asparagus, boil water. As it heats up, it finishes with clean and trim asparagus. Leave or cut in half as whole stalks. Place in boiling water and cook (about 10 minutes) until soft-crisp.6. After removing peppers and tomatoes from the oven, let them cool down (about 2-3 minutes). Place in a bleender, add vinegar and blend until the consistency of applesauce.

7.On a plate with salmon on top, arrange the asparagus.

8.Add salt and pepper to taste.

Tuna Nicoise salad

Total time: 10 minutes

Serve: 4

Ingredients:

- 4tsp. olive oil
- 3 tbsp. balsamic-vinegar
- 2 garlic-cloves (minced)
- 6 cups-mixed greens
- 2 cups string-beans (steamed until just tender)
- 1 cup grape-tomatoes (halved)
- 6 hardboiled eggs (sliced)
- 2, 7 oz. cans-of-tuna

Instructions:

1.Whisk together olive oil, garlic, and vinegar.

2.Prepare a bed of mixed greens. Layer with string beans, tomatoes, egg slices, and tuna. Drizzle with oil mixture.

Ancho tilapia on cauliflower rice

Total time: 30 minutes

Serve: 4

Ingredients:

- 2 lb. tilapia
- 1 tsp. lime juice
- 1tsp. salt
- 1 tbsp. ground ancho pepper (or 1 tbsp. of curry powder)
- 1 tsp. cumin
- 1½ olive oil
- ¼ cup toasted pumpkin seeds
- 6 cups cauliflower rice
- 1 cup fresh coriander (chopped)

Instructions:

1.Preheat oven to 450°F.

2.Take the tilapia and season it with lime juice, and then set on the side.

3.Take a bowl and combine salt, ancho pepper, and cumin. Season the tilapia with the spice mixture.

4.On a baking sheet, arrange the tilapia and bake for 7 minutes.

5.Meanwhile, take a pan and sweat the cauliflower rice in olive oil until tender (about 2 minutes).

6.Mix in the pumpkin seeds and the coriander into the cauliflower rice. Remove from heat, and serve with tilapia.

Salmon Florentine

Total time: 35 minutes

Serve: 4

Ingredients:

- ½ cup green onions (chopped)
- 1 tsp. olive oil
- 2 garlic cloves (minced)
- 1, 12 oz. frozen chopped spinach (thawed and patted dry)
- 1½ cups cherry tomatoes (chopped)
- ¼ tsp. red pepper flakes (crushed)
- ¼ tsp. salt
- ¼ tsp. black pepper
- ½ cup ricotta cheese (part-skim)
- 4, 5½ oz. salmon fillets
- cooking spray

Instructions:

1.Preheat oven to 350°F.

2.Take a pan, cook green onions in olive oil until they begin to soften (about 2 minutes). Add garlic and cook 1 minute more. Add the spinach, tomatoes, red pepper flakes, salt, and pepper. Cook, stirring for 2 minutes. Take of from heat and let it cool for 10 minutes. Then, mix in the ricotta cheese.

3.Then, take the salmon fillets and place a quarter of the spinach mixture on top of them. On a lightly greased sheet, arrange the salmon fillets and bake until salmon is cooked through (about 15 minutes).

Light tuna casserole

Total time: 45 minutes

Serve: 2

Ingredients:

- 1 cup almond milk (unsweetened)
- 4 wedges of garlic and herb cheese (low-fat)
- 1 cup shredded cheddar cheese (low-fat)
- 1 tbsp. chives
- ¼ tsp. cayenne pepper
- 1, 5 oz. can drained tuna packed in water
- 2 cups cooked spaghetti squash
- salt to taste
- black pepper to taste

Instructions:

1.Preheat oven to 350°F.

2.Take a pan and heat almond milk, then add cheese and stir until they melt and the sauce thickens up. Add the rest of the ingredients, leaving some of the cheddar cheese to sprinkle on top.

3.Spread everything in a casserole dish, sprinkle cheese on top and bake for about 30 minutes.

Curry crusted salmon with chili braised cabbage

Total time: 30 minutes

Serve: 4

Ingredients:

- 4, 6 oz. salmon fillets (raw, skinless)
- ¼ tsp. salt
- 1½ tbsp. curry powder
- 1¼ lb. cabbage (trimmed and chopped into bite-sized pieces)
- 2 tsp. fresh ginger root (minced)
- 1 cup chicken broth
- ¼ tsp. red pepper flakes
- 2 green onions (minced)

Instructions:

1.Preheat oven to 425°F.

2.Take the salmon fillets and rub the salt over them until dissolved. Let the fillets sit for 5 minutes

3.Take a plate, spread the curry powder, and then roll each salmon fillet in the curry powder until evenly coated.

4.Place salmon on a baaking sheet and bake for about 8-10 minutes.

5.Meanwhile, cut the cabbage into bite-sized pieces and put it on the side.

6.Take a pan, combine the chicken broth and ginger, and bring to a boil. Add the red pepper flakes and cabbage, cover, and bring to a boil. Reduce heat and simmer until-cabbage is tender (about 3,3-5,3 minutes).

7.Mix the green onions in with the cabbage. Serve salmon on a bed of cabbage.

Shrimp ceviche

Total time: 70 minutes

Serve: 4

Ingredients:

- 2 lb. shrimp (raw, peeled, and deveined)
- ¼ cup lemon juice
- ¼ cup lime juice
- ½ cup fresh tomatoes (diced)
- ½ cup cucumbers (diced)
- 1 jalapeño (seeds removed, diced)
- 1 large red bell pepper (diced)
- ¼ cup green onion (diced)
- ½ cup fresh coriander (chopped)
- 1 avocado
- 4 cups mixed greens-hot sauce

Instructions:

1.Make a big pot of water boil. Immerse the shrimp in boiling water and cook for a period of one to two minutes (depending on the size of the shrimp). Remove it with a slotted spoon from the bath.

2.Place the shrimp in a ceramic or glass tub. Add lemon and lime juice to the mixture. Cover for at least 30 minutes and refrigerate.

3. Combine the shrimp with the onions, cucumbers and peppers. Refrigerate until ready to serve or for at least 33 minutes.

4. Combine the bits of green onion, coriander, and avocado.

5.Serve over a bed of mixed greens. Top with green hot sauce, if desired.

Cajun shrimp sausage and vegetable skillet

Total time: 10 minutes

Serve: 6

Ingredients:

- 28 oz. cooked shrimp
- 12 oz. turkey sausage
- 3 cups zucchini (sliced)
- 3 cups yellow squash
- 1 cup asparagus
- 2 cups red bell pepper
- ¼ tsp. salt
- ½ tsp. black pepper
- 2 tbsp. olive oil
- 2 tbsp. Cajun seasoning

Instructions:

1. Take a bowl and mix in the shrimp, zucchini, sausage, yellow squash, bell pepper, asparagus, and salt and pepper. Add olive oil and cajun-seasoning and toss until well coated.

2. Add to a pan and put on medium heat; cook until the shrimp is pink and the vegetables are tender (about 5-7 minutes).

Parmesan garlic shrimp zucchini noodles

Total time: 20 minutes

Serve: 4

Ingredients:

- 16 oz. frozen uncooked shrimp
- 1 cup cherry tomatoes (halved)
- 8 cups zucchini noodles (3 medium zucchini)
- 3 tbsp. olive oil (divided)
- 2 tbsp. garlic (minced, divided)
- ½ cup grated Parmesan cheese
- 1 tsp. dried oregano
- ½ tsp. chili powder
- ½ tsp. salt
- ½ tsp. black pepper

Instructions:

1.Preheat the oven to 400 degrees. Line a large sheet pan with foil.

2.In a colander, position the frozen shrimp and run cool water over them to thaw (approximately 5 minutes).

3. Toss the parmesan cheese, oregano, chili powder, salt and pepper together.

4. Using a paper towel, drain the shrimp and pat them dry. Put a bowl in it. Uh, pour 1 tbsp. Petroleum, and 1 tbsp. Shrimp with garlic and stir to cover.

5.Sprinkle ½ the cheese mixture on the shrimp and stir to coat. Sprinkle on top with the remaining cheese and keep stirring. Put the shrimp onto the pan and spread out, so they are lying flat. Place in the oven for about 8-10 minutes.

6.Pour the remaining oil and garlic into a large pan, heat for 1 minute, and then stir in the zucchini noodles and tomatoes. Toss to coat. Keep stirring and tossing the noodles as they saute for about 6-8 minutes.

7.Serve the hot veggies and shrimp right away. Sprinkle with extra parmesan cheese, if desired.

Garlic and herb squash stir fry

Total time: 10 minutes

Serve: 1

Ingredients:

- ¾ cup zucchini (sliced)
- ¾ cup yellow squash (sliced)
- 7 oz. cooked shrimp
- 1 tbsp. butter (low-fat)
- 2 tbsp. water
- ½ tsp Mrs. garlic and herb seasoning
- 1 tbsp. grated parmesan cheese (low-fat)
- dash of salt or pepper
- cooking spray

Instructions:

1.Take a pan and spray some cooking spray, then put over medium-high heat and melt butter.

2.Attach the veggies and fry until the veggies are tender-crisp for several minutes.

3.Add shrimp, water, and seasonings. Cover and simmer until desired doneness (usually it takes 4-5 minutes).

4.Sprinkle with parmesan cheese. Serve.

Naked salmon burgers with sriracha mayo

Total time: 20 minutes

Serve: 4

Ingredients:

- 3 tbsp. mayonnaise (light, with olive oil)
- 1 tbsp. sriracha
- ¼ cup red bell pepper (diced)
- ¼ cup yellow bell pepper (diced)
- 6 tbsp. whole-wheat breadcrumbs
- 1 clove garlic (minced)
- 1 lb. salmon fillet
- 1 egg (lightly beaten)
- ½ tbsp. soy sauce
- 1 tsp. lemon juice
- ¼ tsp. salt
- cooking spray
- 4 cups baby arugula
- 4 oz. avocado (sliced)

Instructions:

1.Combine mayonnaise and sriracha and put it on the side.

2.Remove the skin-from the salmon and cut about a 4 oz. Piece off.

3.Place in a food-processor to finely chop. With a knife, finely chop the remaining salmon.

4.Take a bowl combine and the salmon with the bell peppers, whole-wheat breadcrumbs, and garlic.

5.In another bowl, combine egg, soy sauce, lemon juice, and salt, and then add to the salmon mixture, tossing gently to combine.

6.Form 4 patties and refrigerate at least one hour (in this way, burgers become firm and hold together during cooking).

7.Lightly coat a grill-pan with cooking spray. Place over medium-high heat until hot. Cook the patties until cooked through(about 4-5 minutes each side).

8.Place arugula on each plate, top each with a salmon burger, 1 tbsp, mayo, and avocado slices.

Salmon and Cream Cheese Bites

Prep time: 10 min

Cook Time: 10 min

Serving: 2

Ingredients:

- 3 medium eggs
- ¼ teaspoon salt or to taste
- ½ teaspoon dried dill
- 0.88 ounce fresh or smoked salmon, chopped ½ cup cream
- 0.88-ounce grated parmesan
- 0.88-ounce cream cheese, diced

Instructions:

1.Grease 18 wells of a mini muffin pan with some fat.

2.Make sure to preheat your oven to 130 C.

3.Add eggs into a bowl and whisk well. Add salt and cream and whisk well.

4.Add parmesan, cream cheese, and dill and stir.

5.Divide the egg mixture into the 18 wells of the mini muffin pan.

6.Drop at least 1 - 2 pieces of salmon in each well.

7.Place the mini muffin pan and bake for about 12 - 15 minutes or until set in the oven.

8.Cool the mini muffins on your countertop.

9.Remove them from the molds and serve.

Shrimp and Endives

Prep time: 5 min

Cook Time: 12 min

Serving: 2

Ingredients:

- 1 pound shrimp, peeled and deveined
- 2 tablespoons avocado oil
- 2 spring onions, chopped
- 2 endives, shredded
- 1 tablespoon balsamic vinegar
- 1 tablespoon chives, minced
- A pinch of salt and black-pepper from the sea

Instructions:

1.Over medium-high heat, heat a pan with the oil, add the spring onions, endives and chives, stir and cook for 4 minutes.

2.Add the shrimp and remaining ingredients, toss, cook for 8 more minutes over medium heat, divide into bowls and serve.

Nutrition: Calories 378, Fat 2, Carbs 6, Protein 6, Sodium 290

Baked Fish Fillets

Prep time: 5 min

Cook Time: 20 min

Serving: 2

Ingredients:

- 2 tablespoons butter, melted
- A pinch of ground paprika
- 3 fish fillets (5 ounces)
- Pepper to taste
- 1 tablespoon lemon juice
- ½ teaspoon salt

Instructions:

1.Ensure that your oven is preheated to 350 ° F. By greasing it with some fat, prepare a pan for baking. Sprinkle the fillets with salt and pepper and put them in the pan. In a cup, add the butter, paprika and lemon juice and stir. Brush over the fillets with this mixture. In the oven, put the baking pan and cook the fillets.

Nutrition: Calories 245, Fat 12, Carbs 4, Protein 32, Sodium 455

Salmon Cakes

Prep time: 10 min

Cook Time: 10 min

Serving: 2

Ingredients:

- 2 cans salmon (14.75 ounces each), drained
- 8 tablespoons collagen
- 2 cups shredded mozzarella cheese
- 1 teaspoon onion powder
- 4 large pastured egg
- 4 teaspoons dried dill
- 1 pink sea salt teaspoon or to taste
- 4 tablespoons bacon grease

Instructions:

1.Add salmon, collagen, mozzarella, onion powder, eggs, dill, and salt into a bowl and mix well.

2.Make 8 patties from the mixture.

3.Place a large skillet with bacon grease over a medium-low flame.

4.Place the salmon cakes in the skillet once the fat is well heated and cook until it becomes golden brown on all sides.

5.Take off the pan from heat and let the patties remain in the cooked fat for 5 minutes. Serve.

Nutrition: Calories 204, Fat 10, Carbs 5, Protein 29, Sodium 643

Grilled Split Lobster

Prep time: 10 min

Cook time: 15 min

Serving: 2

Ingredients:

- 4 tablespoons olive oil or melted butter Kosher salt to taste
- 4 live lobsters (1 ½ pound each)
- Freshly ground pepper to taste
- Melted butter to serve
- Hot sauce like Frank's hot sauce, to serve Lemon wedges to serve

Instructions:

1.For 15 minutes, put the live lobsters in the freezer.

2.Place them on your cutting board with the belly down on the cutting board. Hold the tail. Split the lobsters in half lengthwise. Start from the point where the tail joins the body and goes up to the head. Flip sides and cut it lengthwise via the tail.

3.Rub melted butter on the cut part immediately after cutting it. Sprinkle salt and pepper over it.

4.Set up your grill and preheat it to high heat for 5-10 minutes. Clean the grill grate and lower the heat to low heat.

5.Place the lobsters on the grill and press the claws on the grill until cooked— grill for 6-8 minutes.

6.Flip sides and cook until it is cooked through and lightly charred.

7.Transfer to a plate. Drizzle melted butter on top and serve.

Nutrition: Calories 433, Fat 4, Carbs 26, Protein 6, Sodium 455

Fish Bone Broth

Prep time: 10 min

Cook time: 4 hrs

Serving: 2

Ingredients:

- 2 pounds of the fish head or carcass
- Salt to taste
- 7 – 8 quarts water + extra to blanch
- 2 inches ginger, sliced
- 2 tablespoons lemon juice

Instructions:

1.To blanch the fish: Add water and fish heads into a large pot. Place the pot over high heat.

2.Turn the heat off when it boils and discard the water.

3.Place the fish back in the pot. Pour 7-8 quarts of water.

4.Place the pot over high heat. Add ginger, salt, and lemon juice.

5.Reduce the heat as the mixture boils, and cover it with a lid.

6.Remove from heat. When it cools down, strain into a large jar with a wire mesh strainer.

7.Refrigerate for 5-6 days. Unused broth can be frozen.

Nutrition: Calories 254, Fat 4, Carbs 26, Protein 6, Sodium 455

Garlic Butter Shrimp

Prep time: 10 min

Cook Time: 10 min

Serving: 2

Ingredients:

- 1 cup unsalted butter, divided
- Kosher salt to taste
- ½ cup chicken stock
- Freshly ground pepper to taste
- ¼ cup chopped fresh parsley leaves
- 3 pounds medium shrimp, peeled, deveined garlic
- Juice of 2 lemons

Instructions:

1.Add 4 tablespoons butter into a large skillet and place the skillet over medium-high flame. Once butter melts, stir in salt, shrimp, and pepper and cook for 2 - 3 minutes. Stir every minute or so. Remove the shrimp with a spoon and place it on a tray.

2.Add garlic into the pot and cook until you get a nice aroma. Pour lemon juice and stock and stir.

3.Lower the heat and cook until the stock falls to half its initial volume until it comes to a boil.

4.Add the rest of the butter, a tablespoon each time, and stir until it melts each time.

5.Add shrimp and stir lightly until well coated.

6.Sprinkle parsley on top and serve.

Nutrition: Calories 484, Fat 21, Carbs 4, Protein 33, Sodium 370

Grilled Shrimp

Prep time: 10 min

Cook Time: 5 min

Serving: 2

Ingredients:

Shrimp Seasoning

- 2 teaspoons garlic powder
- 2 teaspoons Italian seasoning
- 2 teaspoons kosher salt
- ½ - 1 teaspoon cayenne pepper

Grilling

- 4 tablespoons extra-virgin olive oil
- 2 pounds shrimp, peeled, deveined
- 2 tablespoons fresh lemon juice
- Oil to grease the grill grated

Instructions:

1.You can grill the shrimp in a grill or boil it in an oven. Choose whatever method suits you and preheat the grill or oven to high heat.

2.In case you are broiling it in an oven, prepare a baking sheet by lining it with foil and greasing the foil as well, with some fat.

3.Add garlic powder, cayenne pepper, salt, and Italian seasoning into a large bowl and mix well.

4.Add lemon juice and oil and mix well.

5.Stir in the shrimp. Make sure that the shrimp are well coated with the mixture.

6.If using the grill, fix the shrimp on skewers; else, place them on the baking sheet.

7.Grease the grill grates with some oil. Grill the shrimp or broil them in an oven until they turn pink. It should take 180 seconds for each side.

Nutrition: Calories 309, Fat 12, Carbs 8, Protein 16, Sodium 340

Garlic Ghee Pan-Fried Cod

Prep time: 5 min

Cook Time: 10 min

Serving: 2

Ingredients:

- 2 cod fillets (4.8 ounces each)
- 3 cloves garlic, peeled, minced
- Salt to taste
- 1 ½ tablespoons ghee
- ½ tablespoon garlic powder (optional)

Instructions:

1.Place a pan over medium-high flame. Add ghee.

2.Once ghee melts, stir in half the garlic and cook for about 6 – 10 seconds.

3.Add fillets and season with garlic powder and salt.

4.Soon the color of the fish will turn white. This color should be visible for about half the height of the fish.

5.Turn the fish over and cook, adding remaining garlic.

6.When the entire fillet turns white, remove it from the pan.

Nutrition: Calories 193, Fat 16, Carbs 6, Protein 21, Sodium 521

Mussel And Potato Stew

Prep time: 10 min

Cook Time: 20 min

Serving: 2

Ingredients:

- potatoes
- broccoli
- olive oil
- filets
- garlic

Instructions:

1.Submerge potatoes in cold water in a medium saucepan. Put the salt, and boil. Allow cooling for 15 minutes till soft. Let drain.

2.Boil a saucepan of salted water. Put broccoli rabe, and allow to cook till just soft; it should turn bright green. Drain thoroughly, and slice into 2-inch lengths.

3.In a big, deep skillet, mix garlic, anchovies, and oil. Let cook over high heat for approximately a minute, crushing anchovies. In a skillet, scatter the mussels, put chopped parsley, broccoli rabe, and potatoes on top. Put half cup water, and add salt to season.

Place the cover, and allow to cook till mussels are open.

Nutrition: Calories 254, Fat 9, Carbs 12, Protein 11, Sodium 326

Tuna and Tomatoes

Prep time: 5 min

Cook time: 20 min

Serving: 2

Ingredients:

- 1 yellow onion, chopped
- 1 tablespoon olive oil
- 1 pound tuna fillets, boneless, skinless, and cubed
- 1 cup tomatoes, chopped
- 1 red pepper, chopped
- 1 teaspoon sweet paprika
- 1 tablespoon coriander, chopped

Instructions:

1.Over medium heat, heat a pan with the oil, add the onions and pepper and cook for 5 minutes.

2.Add the fish and the other ingredients, cook everything for 15 minutes, divide between plates and serve.

Nutrition: Calories 215, Fat 2, Carbs 34, Protein 16, Sodium 350

Low Carb Shakshuka

Prep Time: 15 minutes

Cook Time: 40 minutes

Serve: 4

Ingredients:

- 2 tablespoons EVOO- extra virgin olive oil 4 teaspoons crushed garlic
- 1 red pepper seeds and pith removed, diced 1 onion finely chopped
- 2 teaspoons turmeric
- 1 little spoon ground coriander 1 teaspoon ground cumin
- 5 teaspoon ground cinnamon
- 3 tablespoons Harissa homemade or store-bought 2 medium tomatoes chopped
- 400 grams /14 oz diced tomatoes no added sugar 8 eggs
- 200 grams /7 oz diced feta cheese salt and pepper to taste fresh coriander to garnish

Instructions:

1.In a big sauté pan, heat 2 tablespoons olive oil and sauté the onion for a few minutes.

2.Add the garlic, turmeric, coriander, cumin, cinnamon, and harissa and sauté for another minute.

3.Add the red pepper and the diced tomatoes and simmer for 20 minutes until the sauce thickens.

4.Make 8 little wells in the sauce, crack the eggs into the well, and season with salt and pepper.

5. Put a lid on the pan and cook for a bit gently for 8-10 minutes, or until the eggs are just set.

6.Place one egg on each serving plate and sprinkle with feta.

7.Spoon over the sauce and garnish with fresh coriander.

Nutrition: Energy (calories): 7621 kcal Protein: 252.86 g Fat: 331.54 g Carbohydrates: 1007.48 g Calcium, Ca7721 mg Magnesium, Mg861 mg Phosphorus, P6091 mg

Thai Cashew Chicken

Prep Time: 10 minutes

Cook Time: 15 minutes

Serve: 4

Ingredients:

- 200 grams of chicken breast, 1 tbsp., cut into bite-sized bits. Flour cassava or all-purpose flour
- 1/3 cup cooking oil with a natural flavour (I used sunflower oil for frying everything)
- For 1 tbsp. Crushed and sliced garlic (I used about 4 cloves)
- 1/2 cup of yellow onions, cut into wedges (1 small onion I used) 1/3 cup of dry red chilies from Thai birds' eye, deep-fried
- 1/2 cup raw unsalted cashew nuts
- 1/3 cup of fresh, thinly julienned, long red chili peppers (I used red spur chilies)
- 1/3 cup of fresh chili peppers from the banana, cut into thin strips
- Seasoning sauce: 1/3 cup green onions (spring onions), cut into 2.5 cm bits.
- For 1 tbsp. 1/2 tbsp. mild soy sauce. 1/2 tbsp. dark soy sauce. Sauce of oysters
- Tsp. 1/4. White ground pepper with a pinch of salt
- The sugar pinch
- Oh. 3 tbsp. Water or stock

Instructions:

1.In a large bowl, add in chicken. Add in seasonings (1 tbsp. light soy sauce, 1/2 tbsp. dark soy sauce, 1/2 tbsp. oyster sauce, ground white pepper, ground black pepper, and a pinch of salt and sugar). Toss to coat evenly. Set aside.

2.In another non-stick pan, heat oil on medium-high heat. Pan-fry the chicken until cooked through but still tender and juicy. Set aside. Pan-fry garlic, ginger, and onions until fragrant and onions are translucent. Do not burn. Set aside.

3.Pour-in the leftover oil. Pan-fry cashew nuts, chilies, and chicken. Toss till fragrant.

Nutrition: Energy (calories): 412 kcal Protein: 15.69 g Fat: 33.8 g Carbohydrates: 15.56 g Calcium, Ca62 mg Magnesium, Mg81 mg Phosphorus, P227 mg

Cheesy Pepper Taco Bake

Prep Time: 10 minutes

Cook Time: 30 minutes

Serve: 4

Ingredients:

- 1 lb. 95-97% lean ground beef (chicken or turkey)
- 1T garlic, cumin, paprika, cayenne, salt, black pepper, onion, and parsley
- 1C no sugar added, fresh vegetable salsa plus 4 additional Tablespoons for garnish
- 1 1/2 lbs. fresh peppers (green, red, poblano, your choice) stems removed, cut in half lengthwise, and seeded.
- 1/2 C shredded low-fat-cheddar cheese 4 T Sour Cream

Instructions:

1.Preheat oven to 375 degrees.

2.In a large skillet – brown meat, garlic, spices, and parsley for about 4 min. Over medium heat. Add Fresh salsa and cook for 5 more minutes.

3.Carefully spoon 1/2 cup mixture in each pepper half going up the open side. The goal is to fill up the pepper in an orderly fashion.

4.Pour 1 C of salsa over the stuffed pepper halves in a small baking pan, cover the pepper mixture with the cheese.

5.Bake for about 10-15 min, or until cheese is completely melted.

6.To serve, divide equally into 4 bowls, and pour 1/2 T of sour cream on top of each.

Nutrition: Energy (calories): 362 kcal Protein: 35.6 g Fat: 14.66 g Carbohydrates: 23.03 g Calcium, Ca122 mg Magnesium, Mg84 mg Phosphorus, P397 mg

Summer Shrimp Primavera

Prep Time: 10 minutes

Cook Time: 10 minutes

Serve: 4

Ingredients:

- 4 ounces of uncooked angel pasta for hair
- 8 shrimp jumbo, peeled and deveined
- 6 fresh asparagus spears, cut into 1/4 cup of olive oil and cut into 2-inch pieces.
- 2 cloves of garlic, minced
- 1/2 cup of fresh sliced mushrooms, 1/2 cup of chicken broth
- 1 tiny, peeled, seeded, and diced plum tomato, 1/4 teaspoon of salt
- 1/8 teaspoon of crushed flakes of red pepper
- 1 tablespoon of fresh basil, oregano, thyme and parsley each, 1/4 cup of grated Parmesan cheese

Instructions:

1.In a big-saucepan, cook pasta according to package directions for al-dente pasta; drain.

2.Preheat broiler. Spray a broiler-proof baking dish with nonstick spray. Sprinkle shrimp with salt and pepper. Arrange on a metal baking pan coated with nonstick spray. Broil for two minutes, 4 inches from the sun. Turn shrimp and broil for 2 minutes longer or until done.

3.Cook the pasta until tender in boiling water (1 to 2 minutes). Run under cold water, drain well, and keep warm.

4.In a big/large non-stick skillet, heat the olive oil over a medium-high heat. Add the garlic, asparagus, mushrooms, tomato and chicken broth; heat through. Stir in the pasta and shrimp; cook until it is completely cooked. Season with salt and pepper flakes. Stir herbs into shrimp mixture. Sprinkle with cheese. Serve immediately.

Nutrition: Energy (calories): 291 kcal Protein: 20.7 g Fat: 17.84 g Carbohydrates: 12.43 g Calcium, Ca100 mg Magnesium, Mg39 mg Phosphorus, P229 mg

Pan-Seared Pork Loin and Balsamic Caramelized Onions

Prep Time: 5 minutes

Cook Time: 25 minutes

Serve: 4

Ingredients:

- on stick cooking spray 1 teaspoon garlic
- 1 teaspoons salt
- 1 teaspoon black pepper 1 teaspoon onion
- 1 teaspoons parsley
- 1 1/2 lbs. pork tenderloin (or beef tenderloin, or chicken breasts)

Instructions:

1.Preheat oven to 350 degrees. Lightly spray a shallow baking PanSprinkle salt and pepper with the steaks and put them in a baking pan.

2.Bake until the meat and internal temperature are tender and reaches 150 degrees, approximately 15 to 20 minutes.

3.While meat is cooking, prepare your gravy. In a large skillet, sauté onion and garlic in olive oil for 3 to 4 minutes. Add sugar to the pan and let cook until caramelized. Once onions are caramelized, add balsamic vinegar and butter. Allow this to simmer until onions are very soft. Thickens as it simmers.

4.Brush top of pork loin with olive oil. Place the pan under the broiler for around 1-2 minutes, until the top layer is caramelized.

5.Remove/Take it from the oven and let it rest for 15 minutes.

6.Slice into medallions and top with gravy. Serve.

Nutrition: Energy (calories): 688 kcal Protein: 23.91 g Fat: 61.78 g Carbohydrates: 7.89 g Calcium, Ca29 mg Magnesium, Mg25 mg

Citrus Shrimp & Spinach

Prep Time: 5 minutes

Cook Time: 10 minutes

Serve: 4

Ingredients:

- on stick cooking spray 1 teaspoon garlic
- 1 teaspoons salt
- 1 teaspoon black pepper 1 teaspoon onion
- 1 teaspoons parsley
- 1 1/2 lbs. wild-caught, raw shrimp, cleaned and tails removed
- 6 cups baby spinach greens, arugula greens, beet greens, or a combination

Instructions:

1.Pour the olive oil into a big-skillet over medium heat (you may want to spray your pan with a non-stick cooking spray).

2.In a small bowl, combine the garlic, salt, pepper, onion powder, and parsley. Then sprinkle over the shrimp and leave to rest while you heat.

3.Add one normal spoon of the olive oil; heat for about 1 minute until hot but not scorching. Add shrimp to the pan. Cook, occasionally stirring, until the shrimp are pink and opaque.

Remove from the pan to a plate and serve over a greens bed with additional olive oil and balsamic vinegar.

Nutrition: Energy (calories): 815 kcal Protein: 37.58 g Fat: 4.03 g Carbohydrates: 164.19 g Calcium, Ca118 mg Magnesium, Mg357 mg

Mediterranean Roasted Chicken with Lemon Dill Radishes

Prep Time: 5 minutes

Cook Time: 30 minutes

Serve: 4

Ingredients:

- 2 lbs. chicken thighs (remove skin)
- Pinch Stacey Hawkins Dash of Desperation Seasoning (or garlic, salt, black pepper, onion, and parsley)
- 1 Tablespoon garlic
- 1 Tablespoon marjoram
- 1 Tablespoon basil
- 1 Tablespoon rosemary
- 1 Tablespoon onion

Instructions:

1.Preheat the oven to 350 degrees.

2.Dice onion.

3.Put the chicken in a deep baking dish.

4.Chop the vegetables. Then put them with some oil on the baking dish.

5.Pour all the seasoning.

6.Bake for 30 minutes, then put the radishes.

7.The radishes cook with the chicken.

8.Serve at room temperature.

Nutrition: Energy (calories): 507 kcal Protein: 37.72 g Fat: 37.74 g
Carbohydrates: 1.88 g Calcium, Ca31 mg Magnesium, Mg44 mg
Phosphorus, P362 mg

Pan-Seared Balsamic Chicken and Vegetables

Prep Time: 10 minutes

Cook Time: 13 minutes

Serve: 4

Ingredients:

- 1/4 cup + 2 tablespoons of Italian salad dressing (I recommend using Kraft light Italian; this is the best quality, and it's what I've used) 3 tablespoons of balsamic vinegar
- Honey 1 1/2 tbsp
- 1/8 tsp (more or less to taste) crushed red pepper flakes 1 1/4 lbs. Tenderloins with chicken breast
- 2 Teaspoons of olive oil
- Salt and black pepper freshly ground
- With 1 lb. New asparagus, cut with tough ends, cut into two-inch sections (look for thinner stalks. Green beans are another good option)
- 1 1/2 cups of matchstick-carrots, 1 cup of grape tomatoes, half the grape tomatoes

Instructions:

1.Combine 1/4 cup of the Italian dressing, 2 Tbsp balsamic vinegar, honey, 1/8 tsp red pepper flakes in a bowl. Put the chicken from the tenderloin package into a big zip-top baggie and pour the marinade over the top.

2.Preheat the oven to 400 degrees.

3.Heat the oil in a pan. Preheat the broilerBegin to add the asparagus to the pan once the oil is hot.

4.Season with salt & pepper and cook only until barely tender, about 3 mins. Remove from skillet and set aside. Add the tomatoes, carrots, and chicken to the pan and continue sautéing for an additional 5-6 mins. (Or until most chicken pieces are lightly browned on both sides)

5. Remove/take the pan (from the heat), and pour over the chicken mixture with the second tablespoon of balsamic vinegar. Cover and place with a lid in the 400-degree oven for an additional 5 mins or until the chicken is completely cooked through.

6.Add the cooked asparagus and the remaining tablespoons of dressing right before serving.

Nutrition: Energy (calories): 439 kcal Protein: 32.85 g Fat: 23.26 g Carbohydrates: 25.5 g Calcium, Ca66 mg Magnesium, Mg61 mg Phosphorus, P332 mg

Tex-Mex Seared Salmon

Prep Time: 5 minutes

Cook Time: 15 minutes

Serve: 4

Ingredients:

- 1 1/2 pounds wild-caught salmon filet (will cook best if you have it at room temp)
- 1 Tablespoon salt
- 1 Tablespoon pepper
- 1Tablespoon garlic
- 1 Tablespoon cumin
- 1 Tablespoon paprika
- 1 Tablespoon cayenne
- 1 Tablespoon onion to taste

Instructions:

- Wash your salmon filet, then cut a 6-inch slit across the middle of the fillet (I use a sandwich knife to make the slit)
- In a bowl, mix-all the ingredients, then rub your mixture in the filet, let it sit for 10-15min
- HEAT OIL TO MEDIUM HIGH
- Sautéed your filet on both sides till it has a nice dark sear; best to use tongs, be careful it is hot!

Nutrition: Energy (calories): 279 kcal Protein: 44.26 g Fat: 9.09 g Carbohydrates: 6.47 g Calcium, Ca46 mg Magnesium, Mg73 mg Phosphorus, P513 mg

Charred Sirloin with Creamy Horseradish Sauce

Prep Time: 5 minutes

Cook Time: 15 minutes

Serve: 4

Ingredients:

- 1 1/2 pounds sirloin steaks, trimmed & visible fat removed 1/2 Tablespoon salt
- 1/2 Tablespoon pepper
- 1/2 Tablespoon garlic and onion to taste 6 Tablespoons low-fat sour cream
- 1-3 T horseradish (from the jar)

Instructions:

1.Preheat oven to high broil

2.Season your steaks with salt, pepper, garlic, and onion, and then place on a cookie sheet lined with foil.

3.Place your sheet on the top rack of your oven and broil until the steaks are charred to your desired doneness. The steaks will also continue to cook once they are removed from the oven.

4.Remove steaks from the oven and let them rest for a few minutes.

5.Warm-up your horseradish sauce in the microwave and set aside.

6.Meanwhile, in a medium saucepan over medium-high heat, warm up the cream, horseradish, and Worcestershire sauce. Whisk constantly until it is warm and remove from heat.

7.Spoon your horseradish sauce over top of your steak and serve immediately.

Nutrition: Energy (calories): 218 kcal Protein: 35.2 g Fat: 6.38 g Carbohydrates: 2.77 g Calcium, Ca50 mg Magnesium, Mg50 mg Phosphorus, P392 mg

Rosemary Beef Tips and Creamy Fauxtatoes

Prep Time: 5 minutes

Cook Time: 30 minutes

Serve: 4

Ingredients:

- 1 1/2 lbs. top sirloin steak, cubed into 1 chunk 1 T (one capful) fresh rosemary
- 1 T (one capful) sage
- 1 T (one capful) black pepper
- 1 T (one capful) onion and garlic 2 1/2 C low sodium beef broth
- 4 C sliced baby portobello mushrooms 1 T fresh minced garlic,
- 1 T (one capful) scallions 1 teaspoon salt and pepper
- 1/2 tsp guar gum & 1/4 C water 2 C hot cauliflower mashed potatoes

Instructions:

1.Note: To speed up the preparation, all ingredients except steak, mushrooms, and a hint of olive oil for searing/cooking can be pre-chopped and stored in baggies ahead of time.

2.In a big-pot, cook beef over medium to high heat. Add onion, garlic, and mushrooms. Stir occasionally. Add oregano, thyme, parsley, salt, and pepper. Stir.

3.Add chopped rosemary, sage, black pepper, and garlic powder. Stir. Add beef broth. Bring to boil. Lower the heat to simmer.

4.Add half the cooked mushrooms into the pot on top and alongside the beef.

5.When beef is cooked to medium-rare, remove from pan and keep warm. Strain broth into a measuring cup to get 4 1/2 cups of broth. Pour broth into a large mixing bowl.

6.Discard solids. Add cornstarch and salt to hot broth and whisk. Add guar gum (or other thickeners) and water and whisk.

7.Bring the water to a boil.

8.Add additional mushrooms and cooked beef to the gravy. Mix.
9.Add chopped garlic and green onions. Mix. Serve sauce alongside beef.

Nutrition: Energy (calories): 492 kcal Protein: 47.47 g Fat: 23.56 g Carbohydrates: 26.14 g Calcium, Ca106 mg Magnesium, Mg70 mg Phosphorus, P606 mg

Balsamic-Glazed Chicken Thighs with Broccoli

Prep Time: 5 minutes

Cook Time: 20 minutes

Serve: 4

Ingredients:

- 4 (~6 ounces) boneless, skinless chicken thighs
- 2 teaspoons (one capful) salt and pepper, garlic, onion, and parsley
- 4 Tablespoons balsamic reduction
- 1/4 C low sodium chicken broth
- 4 C broccoli florets, lightly steamed (crisp-tender) nonstick cooking spray

Instructions:

1.Mix the chicken thighs to coat with salt, pepper, garlic, onion, and parsley, in a medium bowl. Spray a nonstick skillet loosely with cooking spray to reduce the amount of fat absorbed into the thighs. Heat the skillet to medium-high.

2. Cook and add the thighs to the skillet, uncovered, for about 6 minutes on each side until browned and no longer pink inside.

3.Add the balsamic reduction to deglaze the pan, and cook for one minute. Put the chicken and balsamic reduction into the slow cooker.

4. Turn the slow-cooker to high and add the chicken broth. Cook for 15 minutes or until the chicken is tender enough to pull apart with a fork. Stir in the broccoli florets and cook with the chicken for extra 5 minutes or until the broccoli is cooked through but still crisp.

5.Serve hot with a side of wild rice and chopped green onion.

Nutrition: Energy (calories): 823 kcal Protein: 44.87 g Fat: 26.37 g Carbohydrates: 100.81 g Calcium, Ca172 mg Magnesium, Mg121 mg Phosphorus, P476 mg

Chicken with Lemon Caper Butter Sauce

Prep Time: 10 minutes

Cook Time: 5 minutes

Serve: 4

Ingredients:

- 2 Chicken breasts
- low sodium pink Himalayan salt Black pepper
- 2 normal spoon extra-virgin olive oil 1 teaspoon minced garlic
- 1/2 cup unsalted chicken broth or stock 1/3 cup dry white wine
- 1/4 cup low sodium capers, rinsed and drained Juice from one lemon
- Lemon slices for garnish
- 2 Tablespoon parsley, for garnish

Instructions:

1.Set aside and season the chicken breast with salt and pepper.

2. Heat olive oil for 10 seconds in an instant pot in sauté mode. Add garlic and sauté for 10 seconds.

3.Add chicken broth or stock, white wine, capers, and lemon juice. Press cancel and close lid with a vent in sealing position. Cook on manual mode for 5 minutes.

4.When the instant pot beeps, do a 5-minute natural pressure release.

5.Drain chicken and place it on the cutting board. Use two forks to shred chicken into chunks.

6.Gently stir in the pan sauce and return to the instant pot. Add 1/2 cup of water or chicken bone broth.

7.Press sauté mode and bring to a boil for 2 minutes, stirring occasionally. Add lemon slices and parsley and serve.

Nutrition: Energy (calories): 326 kcal Protein: 32.76 g Fat: 18.52 g Carbohydrates: 6.42 g Calcium, Ca78 mg Magnesium, Mg43 mg Phosphorus, P301 mg

Tender Taco Chicken

Prep Time: 5 minutes

Cook Time: 10 minutes

Serve: 4

Ingredients:

- 1 1/2 pounds boneless, skinless-chicken breast 1 Tablespoon, low salt Tex-Mex seasoning
- 1/2 C fresh chopped tomatoes or low carb, no sugar added salsa 1 tsp Stacey Hawkins Dash of Desperation Seasoning
- Your favorite on-program taco condiments

Instructions:

1.Cutting the chicken into 1/2-inch strips and sprinkle with the Tex Mex and dash of desperation seasoning.

2.In a large pan, heat the over medium and sauté the chicken for about 10 minutes, until cooked through and no longer pink.

3.Remove to a bowl and add tomatoes or salsa and toss to combine.

Nutrition: Energy (calories): 325 kcal Protein: 16.43 g Fat: 10.65 g Carbohydrates: 40.05 g Calcium, Ca47 mg Magnesium, Mg41 mg Phosphorus, P169 mg

Garlic Crusted Baby Back Ribs

Prep Time: 15 minutes

Cook Time: 1-hour

Serve: 2

Ingredients:

- 11 and 3/4 rack baby back ribs
- 2 tablespoon extra-virgin olive oil Kosher salt and freshly ground pepper 6 clove garlic
- 12 sprig thyme
- 8 sage leaves with stems 2 sprig rosemary

Instructions:

1.For the ribs, trim the excess fat and slice down the middle into one and a half-inch sections. Add olive-oil and season with salt and pepper.

2.Lay the food grilling rack over a gas or charcoal grill and grill for 1-hour basting with extra-virgin olive oil and coating each side.

3.And then line it in the middle of the grill for 8 minutes.

4.In the meantime, place the garlic and herbs on a large sheet of foil and wrap it tightly.

5.Transfer the ribs and ragout to a platter and drizzle with juices, and top with the foil's garlic and herbs.

Nutrition: Energy (calories): 19328 kcal Protein: 1710.36 g Fat: 1364.22 g Carbohydrates: 76.49 g Calcium, Ca1726 mg Magnesium, Mg2093 mg

Blistered Tomatoes with Balsamic and Goat Cheese

Prep Time: 5 minutes

Cook Time: 10 minutes

Serve: 12

Ingredients:

- 9 oz. Mission Organics® Blue Corn Tortilla Chips 16 oz. Cream Cheese
- 8 oz. Goat Cheese
- 1 Clove Garlic, Minced
- ¼ Cup Chives – Fresh, Chopped
- 2 Tbsp. Scallions – Greens Chopped 1 ½ Cups Cherry Tomatoes, Chopped 2 Tbsp. Olive Oil
- 2 Tbsp. Balsamic Vinegar
- Salt and Black Pepper to Taste

Instructions:

1.Preheat the oven to 350°. Lightly grease a 2 ¼ cup ramekin with non-stick canola oil spray. Place 1/3 cup of the chip bag into the ramekin.

2.Preheat oven to 350°. Using an electric-mixer on medium-high speed, combine the cream cheese, 2 oz of the goat cheese, 2 tbsp.

Of the chives, garlic, and scallions. Season with salt and black pepper.

3. Place the ramekin in the oven and cook for about 10 minutes until the mixture starts to bubble. Remove and allow for 5 minutes to cool. Stir in the tomatoes, drizzle with the oil and vinegar, and sprinkle with the remaining goat cheese and chives.

4.Serve with the remaining chips.

Nutrition: Energy (calories): 656 kcal Protein: 20.01 g Fat: 49.1 g Carbohydrates: 34.47 g Calcium, Ca443 mg Magnesium, Mg65 mg Phosphorus, P451 mg

Mediterranean Style Grilled Lamb Burgers

Prep Time: 20 minutes

Cook Time: 10 minutes

Serve: 8

Ingredients:

- 2 lb. ground-lamb or a combination of lamb and beef (see cook's tip #1)
- 1 small-red-onion, grated 2 garlic cloves, minced
- 1 cup chopped fresh-parsley 10 mint leaves, chopped
- 2 and one-half tsp dry oregano 2 tsp ground cumin
- One-half tsp paprika
- One-half tsp cayenne-pepper, optional Kosher salt, and black pepper
- Extra virgin-olive-oil (I used Private Reserve Greek extra virgin olive oil)
- To Serve:
- Warm Greek pita bread or buns Homemade Tzatziki sauce Sliced tomatoes
- Sliced Green bell pepper Sliced cucumbers
- Sliced red onions
- Pitted Kalamata olives, sliced Crumbled feta

Instructions:

1.Combine the ground meat, the onion, the garlic, herbs, and spices in a large mixing bowl and lightly mix with your hands until combined. Do not over mix.

2.Form 8 patties approximately three-fourths inch thick.

3. Brush the olive oil on the outside of the patties and season all sides with salt and pepper.

4.Preheat the grill on medium-high.

5.Cook the patties for 5-6 minutes per side for medium-rare. Well done, burgers can be drier and a bit tougher.

6.Spread 2 Tbsp of Tzatziki sauce on both sides of the pita bread or buns.

7.Place the patties on the pita-bread and top with the sliced kalamata olives, sliced cucumbers, sliced red onions, sliced tomatoes, and grated feta cheese.

8.Wrap the pita bread or buns around the patties and serve.

Nutrition: Energy (calories): 336 kcal Protein: 36.43 g Fat: 17.36 g W Carbohydrates: 8.31 g Calcium, Ca186 mg Magnesium, Mg78 mg Phosphorus, P333 mg

Basil Chicken Sausage & Zucchini Spaghetti

Prep Time: 10 minutes

Cook Time: 10 minutes

Serve: 4

Ingredients:

- 1 normal spoon extra-virgin olive oil, or more as needed 4 chicken sausage links, sliced
- 2 tablespoons minced garlic 1 large tomato, chopped
- 4 zucchinis, spiralized using the 3mm blade and trimmed 1/4 cup chopped fresh basil
- salt and ground black pepper to taste
- 1 pinch-red-pepper flakes, or more to taste 1/4 cup grated Parmesan cheese, or to taste

Instructions:

1.Heat-oil in a large-skillet over medium heat. Add chicken sausage and cook for about 4 minutes, or until lightly browned.

2.Add garlic, tomato, and zucchini noodles and cook until the zucchinis get tender and begin to soften.

3.Stir in basil. Add salt, pepper, and chili.

4.Move the mixture to a bowl and top with parmesan cheese before serving.

Nutrition: Energy (calories): 232 kcal Protein: 18.95 g Fat: 11.75 g Carbohydrates: 14.81 g Calcium, Ca125 mg Magnesium, Mg61 mg Phosphorus, P232 mg

Cheat Kebabs

Prep Time: 10 minutes

Cook Time: 25-35 minutes

Serve: 4

Ingredients:

- 4 C mixed veggies (peppers, zucchini, mushrooms, yellow squash, etc.) chopped into 1 piece
- 1 1/2 pounds (24 oz) chicken breast meat cut into 1" chunks
- 1-2 Tablespoons Garlic Gusto Seasoning or Tuscan Fantasy Seasoning (or lemon, pepper, garlic, onion, parsley, salt & pepper) 4 teaspoons Stacey Hawkins Roasted Garlic Oil (or lemon, pepper, garlic, onion, parsley, salt & pepper)
- 1/4 C apple cider vinegar

Instructions:

1.Preheat the grill to medium-high. {Note: For temps, see grill manufacturer's instructions}. Spray grill with non-stick cooking spray.

2.Cut the veggies into 1 piece.

3.Pat the chicken-dry and season with the Gusto or Tuscan Fantasy or other favorite seasonings. {Note: Try and keep it simple. Salt, pepper, and onion powder work wonderfully}.

4.Pour the vinegar into a shallow bowl.

5.Dip the chicken pieces in the vinegar and then coat with the Gusto or Tuscan Fantasy.

6.Dip the vegetables into the vinegar and then place them on the chicken.

{Note: It is fine if the pieces overlap. We are creating a packet that will deliver wonderful flavors as it cooks. We'll account for the remaining vinegar in the marinade}.

7.Press the veggies and chicken into the Gusto or Tuscan fantasy and really press down hard! Stuff should be touching all surfaces of the chicken.

8.When your grill is smoking, but the kebabs on the grill and over medium-high heat, close the lid and cook for 10-15 minutes and then check to see if the chicken is done.

9.To have the chicken to be a little crispy after it is cooked, place the finished kebabs onto a hot grill for 1 minute just before you serve.

10.Serve with fresh pita and various toppings and the remaining marinade.

Nutrition: Energy (calories): 363 kcal Protein: 38.97 g Fat: 18.84 g Carbohydrates: 8.15 g Calcium, Ca46 mg Magnesium, Mg71 mg Phosphorus, P342 mg

Lemony Roasted Beets

Prep Time: 10 minutes

Cook Time: 20 minutes

Serve: 6

Ingredients:

- 6 Cups red beets cut into three-fourth chunks 1 Tablespoon olive oil
- 1 Tablespoon salt
- 1 Tablespoon pepper
- 1 Tablespoon onion and garlic 1 Tablespoon fresh lemon juice 1/2 cup crumbled feta cheese

Instructions:

1.Preheat oven to 400 degrees F.

2.Sauté the onions, garlic, and lemon juice in the olive oil with salt and pepper for about 3 minutes.

3.After sautéing the onions and lemon juice, spread the beets evenly in a lightly oiled baking dish.

4.Sprinkle the crumbled feta cheese over the beets.

5.Pour the sautéed onions mixture over the beets.

6.Bake the lemony roasted beets for 20 minutes, and serve.

Nutrition: Energy (calories): 206 kcal Protein: 3.84 g Fat: 5.12 g Carbohydrates: 38.82 g Calcium, Ca91 mg Magnesium, Mg39 mg Phosphorus, P87 mg

Creamy Paprika Pork

Prep Time: 10 minutes

Cook Time: 15 minutes

Serve: 4

Ingredients:

- 1 pork-tenderloin (1 pound), cut into 1-inch cubes 1 little spoon all-purpose flour
- 4 little spoons paprika 3/4 teaspoon salt 1/4 teaspoon pepper 1 little spoon butter
- ¾ cup heavy-whipping cream Hot-cooked egg-noodles or rice Minced fresh parsley, optional

Instructions:

1.Preheat oven to 355 F. Coat a large baking dish with vegetable cooking spray. In a bowl, toss pork with flour, paprika, salt, and pepper until coated. Heat butter in a large skillet over medium-high heat until it starts to sizzle.

2.Add pork, sauté for 3 minutes. Add cream; cover and bring to a boil, reduce heat, simmer for 15 minutes.

3.Serve over hot cooked noodles or rice. Sprinkle with parsley if desired.

Nutrition: Energy (calories): 308 kcal Protein: 32.86 g Fat: 17.9 g Carbohydrates: 2.89 g Calcium, Ca40 mg Magnesium, Mg42 mg

Tender & Tangy BBQ Ribs

Prep Time: 15 minutes

Cook Time: 45 minutes

Serve: 6

Ingredients:

- 1/4 C apple-ider-vinegar 1/4 C water
- 2 lbs. boneless-pork ribs, all visible fat trimmed off & discarded 1-2 normal spoons SH Cinnamon Chipotle
- Sugar-Free BBQ Sauce – Mesquite Style (or your favorite)

Instructions:

1.Preheat oven to 350 degrees.

2. Mix the apple cider vinegar with water in a small tub. Place the ribs in a large plastic bag that can be resealed. Pour the apple cider vinegar mixture and the ribs into a plastic jar. Seal the bag and put it for a minimum of 15 minutes in the refrigerator.

3. On a rimmed-baking mat, put the ribs and with a brush, generously coat both sides of the ribs with barbecue sauce. Sprinkle cinnamon chipotle sugar-free syrup on both sides of the ribs.

4.Cook ribs in the preheated 350-degree oven for 45 minutes. Take out and brush with more BBQ sauce. Then place back in the oven for another 5 to 10 minutes.

5.Let it cool for a minute, then serve.

Nutrition: Energy (calories): 221 kcal Protein: 31.49 g Fat: 8.57 g
Carbohydrates: 2.75 g Calcium, Ca53 mg Magnesium, Mg37 mg
Phosphorus, P310 mg

Tender Beef Stew with Rosemary

Prep Time: 20 minutes

Cook Time: 2 hours

Serve: 8

Ingredients:

- 4 slices-cut bacon into thin strips
- After trimming, 4 pounds beef chuck roast bits - cut into 1 1/2 - 2- inch pieces
- 1/2 small spoon of kosher salt I use 1/2 small spoon of black pepper with Morton coarse kosher salt
- 1 1/2 cups chopped onion
- 2 cups of fresh (peeled) or frozen pearl onions
- 2 1/2 cups of peeled carrot pieces and cut into 1 - 1 1/2- inch of 1 tablespoon of oil if necessary3-4 cloves garlic
- 2 sprigs of rosemary
- 4 sprigs of thyme
- 2 bay leaves dried
- Two cups of low-sodium beef broth, two tablespoons of soy sauce
- 2-3 tablespoons of butter, 2-3 tablespoons of flour, softened
- If required, 1/2 teaspoon kosher salt
- 2 tablespoons of chopped fresh flat-leaf parsley – Optional

Instructions:

1.Place the meat in a large mixing bowl. Sprinkle with salt and pepper.

2.In a medium-sized sauté pan put the 2 tablespoons of oil, add the bacon strips. Cook for about 2-3 minutes.

3.Add the onion, carrot, pearl onions (fresh or frozen), garlic cloves, and rosemary springs. Until the vegetables begin to soften, cook for 5-6 minutes.

4.Add the vegetables and bacon to the meat mixture.

5.Add the thyme, bay leaves, and broth.

6.Refrigerate until ready to cook the stew. This can be done a day ahead.

7.After refrigerating the stew, let the stew come to room temperature.

8.Heat the oven to 350 °F.

9.Grease a large baking pan (if needed) and put the meat and vegetables into it.

10.With the gravy, cover the meat and vegetables. Cook for about 90-120 minutes until the meat starts to get tender.

11.Take the meat out of the baking pan and place it on a platter or in a large bowl using 2 forks to shred the pot's meat.

12.Place the meat back in the potting mixture. Add the soy sauce and the butter and stir it.

13.Reduce the heat to medium-low. If the stew starts to get very thick and dry, add a little more broth and stir.

14.Mix the 2 tablespoons of flour with 1/2 cup of water until very thin paste forms. Stir into the stew while whisking regularly. Add a little-extra-water if needed if the stew gets too dry. Add the salt and mustard and mix well at the end.

15.Add the parsley to the stew at the end.

Nutrition: Energy (calories): 474 kcal Protein: 51.48 g Fat: 22.46 g Carbohydrates: 18.46 g Calcium, Ca85 mg Magnesium, Mg64 mg Phosphorus, P520 mg

Glazed Ginger Chicken and Green

Prep Time: 5 minutes

Cook Time: 20-35 minutes

Serve: 4

Ingredients:

- 1 Tablespoon Toasted Sesame Ginger Seasoning
- 1 1/2 pounds boneless-skinless-chicken (breasts or thighs) nonstick cooking spray
- ¼ cup low-sodium soy sauce ½ cup water
- 4 cups fresh green beans, ends snipped

Instructions:

1.Preheat oven to 350F.

2.In a medium bowl, add the chicken, ginger seasoning, and soy sauce. Toss to combine. Marinate at room temperature.

3.Spray a large baking sheet; add the chicken mixture and spread evenly.

4. Place the sheet in the oven on the center rack and roast it for 20 minutes. If desired, baste the chicken with the liquid from the bowl (2- 4 tablespoons) three times while roasting.

5.Remove the baking sheet from the oven.

6.Add the green beans (in the bowl) and water; cover the pan with aluminum foil and bake for 10 to 15 more minutes.

7.Remove the pan and stir the beans. Bake for a further five to seven minutes, or until the beans are fluffy.

8.Serve and sprinkle with some fresh ground pepper.

Nutrition: Energy (calories): 259 kcal Protein: 41.77 g Fat: 6.23 g Carbohydrates: 8.04 g Calcium, Ca77 mg Magnesium, Mg86 mg Phosphorus, P435 mg

Zucchini Pappardelle with Sausage

Prep Time: 5 minutes

Cook Time: 15 minutes

Serve: 4

Ingridients:

- • 1 1/2 lbs. Lean turkey or chicken sausage, seasoned in Italy (your choice is hot or sweet) 2 C chopped tomatoes
- Stacey Hawkins Garlic and Spring Onion Seasoning 1 Tablespoon (1 capful)
- • 4 cups of fresh zucchini noodles (about 3 cups) zucchinis, 8 long)
- 4 teaspoons Olive Oil
- A little bit of Stacey Hawkins Dash of Desperation Seasoning

Instructions:

1.Wash and gently dry zucchini. Cut it lengthwise into spaghetti sized strips; using a vegetable peeler, peel zucchini into thin shreds. Transfer zucchini to a salad spinner. Sprinkle with 1 teaspoon of the olive oil and a Dash of Desperation Seasoning. Toss gently to coat with oil and seasoning.

2.In a skillet, brown sausage; drain fat and transfer sausage to a large pot. Add 2 teaspoons olive oil, chopped tomatoes, and Stacey

Hawkins Garlic and Spring Onion Seasoning. Cook over high heat until tomatoes are softened, about 5 minutes.

3.Fill a large pot with generously salted water. Bring water to boil and cook zucchini pasta for 7 minutes. While you are cooking zucchini, add sausage, tomato, and seasoning combination to the zucchini pasta and cook together on medium heat.

4.Use tongs to submerge zucchini noodles one at a time into a large pot of boiling water with 1 teaspoon olive oil stirred in. Once done, strain it along with other ingredients.

5.Preheat oven to 350 degrees. Transfer all ingredients to a large casserole or baking dish and mix thoroughly. Top dish with fresh grated Parmesan cheese. Bake for about 15 minutes in the preheated oven, until the cheese is bubbly and golden brown.6.This dish is equally delicious served either hot or cold. Serve in a bowl and stir in a little bit of pasta water.

Nutrition: Energy (calories): 801 kcal Protein: 33.31 g Fat: 51.13 g Carbohydrates: 49.95 g Calcium, Ca58 mg Magnesium, Mg41 mg Phosphorus, P321 mg

Lightning Source UK Ltd.
Milton Keynes UK
UKHW050808110521
383453UK00003B/52